SCOUSE BROWS

Madelaine Kinsella

ACKNOWLEDGEMENTS

INTERNATIONAL GARDEN FESTIVAL first appeared in JARG Magazine issue #3.

Earlier versions of the following poems first appeared in Bido Lito!: MOTHER TONGUE, START-RITE MARY JANES, DERT, VETEMENTS, and STREET CATHEDRAL.

I would like to give my thanks to Toria Garbutt and Wrecking Ball Press, for your belief in this work.

To Jeff Young, for your encouragement when I was your student. For your support at the very beginning. The poem LISTED is for you.

To Rachel Walton, for your constant and undying and relentless faith in me. You just get it. You always have.

To Ellie Grendon, Kevanté A.C. Cash, Peter Clarke, Susie Wilson, Sammy Weaver, and all my MA class for your advice and support with many of these poems. For believing in them and for believing in me. To Carol Ann for your teaching and stories.

To Stephanie Gavan and Eavan Seasman for your words, and for being incredible and important Scouse female artists.

To my parents, Eileen, and Kevin, two of North Liverpool's greatest artists, the most resilient people I know.

To Matthew Thomas Smith, for everything.

And finally, to Liverpool, who birthed me, who made me, who I dedicate this pamphlet to.

SCOUSE BROWS
Madelaine Kinsella

ISBN 978-1903110843

First published in this edition 2021 by Wrecking Ball Press.

Cover design: humandesign.co.uk

Supported using public funding by
LOTTERY FUNDED | ARTS COUNCIL ENGLAND

For Liverpool
The hardest nut to crack.

CONTENT

MANAGED DECLINE

Like you, I had the chance, before going off on holiday, of a short talk with my fellow Minister about his forthcoming Merseyside report.   This is obviously not the time for a reaction to the detail of what he will have to suggest.   But there is one short point worth making now.

As you know, I have for some years had some sympathy with his idea of giving several Ministers the responsibility for individual regions.   In the present context it may serve too as a useful reminder of the need to be careful not to over-commit scarce resources to Liverpool.

For reasons which we all understand, I fear that Merseyside is going to be much the hardest nut to crack.   It will be hard to persuade prospective private sector investors to take the opposite view.   Even so we do not want to find ourselves concentrating all the limited cash that may have to be made available into Liverpool and having nothing left for possibly more promising areas such as the West Midlands or, even, the North East.   It would be even more regrettable if some of the brighter ideas for renewing economic activity were to be sown only on relatively stony ground on the banks of the Mersey. I cannot help feeling that the option of managed decline, which the CPRS rejected in its study of Merseyside, is one which we should not forget altogether.   We must not expend all our resources in trying to make water flow uphill.

SCOUSE BROWS

MOTHER TONGUE

At birth I sobbed.
The metal rod, steaming red
branded my tongue, bruised me with flaw,
etched cackles onto my taste buds.

My tongue burns every night. Muscle memory.
In the day she is senseless and sharp.
Asbestos mouth. My vowels wide as w*aiiide*.
Tiny rusted hooks pull my lips taut.

The branding tool scolds us all with accent.
Steel alloy, Celtic and Lancashire.
The midwives keep it in the storage cupboard
between nappies and starched blankets.

I carry this city in my mouth.
Gargle her, spit her out, cough
her up and scrape her off the cobbles.
Cradle her in my tongue curls.

I bring her tv fuzz on every sentence
until each day ends. She is grateful,
and to thank me, she burns.
She burns in the back my throat.

START-RITE MARY JANES

Patent leather. Worn buckle from
weekdays, creasing across her arch.
Pretty little things without grip.
Frictionless dolly shoes.
She doesn't go against the grain.
So well behaved she slips on ice
and doesn't even cry.
Knees like rotting cherries.

Little girls have to learn risk.
To fall and scrape their limbs,
to measure the hardness of the earth
for themselves. As buckles become laces,
they must find the ground
before it claims them first.
To refocus their minds on rescue
and wait for comfort as if it were coming.

STREET CATHEDRAL

This is the word of the city. Thanks be to her. Graffiti sprawled on this derelict building. It's their cathedral. They worship in tag. Aerosol scripture. Biblical attention to detail. Three phrases appropriate the building. A Scally incantation. Father. Son. Holy Spirit.
BRASS. SIX TIMES. CREED.

BRASS. Something the city is as bold as. Another word for prostitute. Derogatory. If you want to be. Brass Knuckles. The fabric of saxophones. She had the brass neck to come up in here. Arfaced. Confident. Arrogant. Women enjoying life like men might do. The audacity. The brass neck.

SIX TIMES. How many times a city's team has won the Champions League at the time of this graffiti. This tag must be fresh. New-born. Nine months. Perhaps premature. They know what unity looks like. Resilience as natural as score boards. The apostles will update the mural when they do it again. They yearn to. Adamant it will need the maintenance.

CREED. Scent of the city. Between sea water. Car fumes. Polly. Two hundred quid aftershave. Jarg versions. Blouse replicas. They all prove popular. Women of the city have learned to sniff the scent out like police dogs at Creamfields. Bitches and their senses. Refuse entry to men who smell like toilette. They want potent. Full proof parfum. Creed. A rhapsody the arl queens chant before bread and wine. The sensation of mass.

Street cathedral. The red brick relic that's survived all the wars thrown at her. She stands and will stand. Covered in tags. In graffiti. Claimed by the city that loves her. Claimed as one of their own.

LIVER BIRDS

I dreamt that me and you were birds.
We could fly anywhere we wanted
and we flew side by side.

When I woke up and realised you were
nowhere to be found I instead found joy
in the grey feather of a bed cushion.

I look outwards, plucking at possible meaning
and you, with your back to me, look in.

VETEMENTS

It's crazy, scary stuff.
But we only see 20% of it.
Perfect freedom to exploit. Identity
politics with a brand-new savage twist.

The same fashion as U.S. prison wear.
Perfect irony in the social media age.
The chunky dad trainer that trend invented;
I feel I want to own it.

The gap between rich and poor,
or whatever you want to call it.
They know what trouble looks like.
In the streets stuff. In the dark places.

Like a bunch of posh kids dressed to riot
with luxury streetwear as their alliance.

Adapted from Sarah Mower's review of Vetements Fall 2019 Menswear
show and in interview with fashion designer Demna Gvasalia.

LISTED

In the city where streets won't shed their
cobblestones, memories pile like landfill.
Kid's accents grow like pains. Like elder.
A gob full of abscess. Tiny protests.

Their voices, overgrown rose bushes.
I am a thorny young woman now. My tongue
uncurls, fresh red buds carrying PRICK.
Petals falling from the trauma.

I've treaded the small of your back
for years as long as Upper Parliament St.
The heel of my shoe grew taller as I did,
and you taught me how to balance.

I still see my reflection in your sandstone.
A baby daughter with a cob on in the docks.
An ice cream has fallen from grip onto the
floor. The child screaming as if melting.

Before I knew Grade Listings protected you,
I played against your red brick walls
ignoring your no ball games tattoo.
I wish I could list every place where we grew.

scour them with concrete   preserve them like rare disgusting bugs   crush their
exoskeletons   press them between legislative journals   the dandelions
buttercups   they are the weeds   dig up their listed buildings   build a cement garden

EDEN

There's worn turn of phrase in the city:
Need to get out of Liverpool, full of snakes.
But there are no snakes. And no one leaves.

Their hang ups slithering behind them
like addiction. Compelled to stay, to blame
incidents on the non-native reptilia.

Few flee, like migrating birds, to Australia
as often as trope. Like Enfield sketches
from the 90s that southerners cling to

for insult. Some *calm down*, to postcodes
with better letters and richer councils
for the cost of a purple wheelie bin.

Everywhere we go, we take ourselves,
us locals. Our city sits like a smoker's
cough in our lungs. Like peristalsis

our accent involuntarily contracts and
constricts language. We give words texture,
new meaning, and the Received, rejected, retaliate

with policy. Cuts to funding. Poverty on purpose.
Striping the city of soul like stale wallpaper.
Cladding us with bin dipper status. But

somewhere a child is born with grit
in their throat. Lying on their spine, relying
on instinct to survive. They must learn and
unlearn all of this.

POLYVINYL CHLORIDE

He *loved* poetry.
Had a bong, but no bookshelf
in his apartment.

DEATH OF A BARONESS

OLÉ! OLÉ! OLÉ! OLÉ!

In classrooms, the schoolboys fidget with betting pens
and disrupt lesson plans. Gaining their interest was simple
as convincing water to run uphill. They are written off
by teachers who cannot understand their accent.

*

Elsewhere, a dying breath, frail as tin
exhaled a siren up the country. A song
only the city could hear. Once heard, the fathers
would wait outside the school gates for their sons
to climb over. They wanted to celebrate together.

*

A cardboard coffin appeared outside the town hall before
the buses finished their routes. The relic must have waited
thirty years for a trampling. The fathers had waited too,
all this time. Now they can share the song with their boys.

*

Outside the town hall, they teach the schoolboys to curl
their tongues around language. To salivate in the spice of aggression.
Bend their mouths to savour distain. How to *howack* and spit, like a man,
on the cobblestones. Like it was the very soil she would return to.
For their efforts, the boys are rewarded with cans and swear words.

*

The fathers were schoolboys when the baroness had power.
Their own fathers, dockers. Their brothers, football fans.
The by-product of wretched policies in the port city.
This would be taught down, son after son. Hatred their heirloom.

*

How glorious death can be if you wait long enough.
The fathers hold their son's heads back and pour the lager
into their mouths like communion. Pleb champagne.
Pyro. They trample on the makeshift coffin now.
Dancing, spilling milk, singing the song only the city can hear.

*

They hold each other still, attaching each other's party hats.
The schoolboys play kazoos, full of ale, until nightfall.
Today they wished for her to have suffered, collective vengeance.
How beautiful unity is to see. How close joy is to terror.

*

The song rings around the city like church bells.
The schoolboys had so much fun at the party,
they say they want to do this again when they are fathers too.
How they wish she would come back and die again.
They'd do it better next time. They'd do it even better.

*

SCOUSE BROWS

Liverpool school girl,
already sussing out who she is,
with dark brown kohl pencil.
A new arch embedded into her face.

Big, orrible slugs. They grow
and grow and consume
her forehead in diameter.
A new shape to fill in.

Uniform codes and not adhering
to uniform codes. Make up remover.
Parched and stale baby wipes.
Never mind, there's always tomorrow.

Uniform codes and not adhering
to uniform codes. She has common
eyebrows. By that they mean:
                    lower band
                    teen pregnancy
                    bad for league table
                    eyebrows

Mr. Stirling and OFSTED don't like her eyebrows.

PE kits in blue JD bags.
The meff box of lost and found.
Lip gloss, cheap body spray, doused in it.
A jarg sick note and an entry way paradise.

A race back to the school gate
before the bell catches her but
it always did. If not sooner babe, then later.
The paled faced Porter, shouting

back to class. Take that make-up off.
Over and over. Term after term.
There's always tomorrow, for the
stubborn bitch with the furrowed brow
and a scowl to match, to try again.

KECKS

He wore tailored kecks.
So nice that I folded them
once they were removed.

THE HONEYBEES ON THE THEATRE ROOF

On a tour of the theatre, they tell us
that they keep bees on the roof. That
their honey has a distinctive taste, as
the bees in the hive, instead of feeding
on flowers, they eat the abandoned sweets
from the pavement of our childhood city.

That evening as we kissed goodnight
as we had done many nights before, I
listened for notes of your being. I felt
on my palate your diet of experience,
trying to gauge your shelf life with my lips.
That evening I tasted your life.

Your mouth, a honeycomb.
My taste buds, a hive, swarming
into you. Vibrating like tiny gramophones.
I want to tell you about my day. To regurgitate
my thoughts into you. And we call that love.
Our ability to eat the past
and make it taste like a future.

DERT

A substance that soils this city.
The state of us girls,
to have dert on our tongues
and no soap to wash it out.

In science I look down my blouse
waiting to become a woman.
To be validated by touch
like the lab rats we dissected.

This makes a girl a dert,
a slut, for wanting, panting.
A woman needs convincing,
coercing, reasonable force.

Boarded up houses mark derty streets.
This is my home. I am the dert,
where women before me have settled
like dust mounting the tv stand.

And from the dert, I will rise.

"Carefully-crafted radical missives from North Liverpool. A vital broadcast."
Matthew Thomas Smith

"These poems are a prism through which the city's wayward spirits are illuminated; jagged and full of nerve. Kinsella walks beside punters-come-prophets and stiff-necked school girls, circling the curses of want. Tending to scoured knees, she sings hymns of the headstrong and hungry, of sandstone and spit, reciting her homeland in a voice as frictive as the asphalt on which this city cuts its teeth."
Stephanie Gavan

"A riveting and necessary poetry collection. From beginning to end, we are left yearning for more, but Kinsella leaves no crumbs behind."
Kevanté A. C. Cash

£6.00

ISBN 978-1-9031108-4-3

WRECKING BALL PRESS

9 781903 110843